Eating Disorder Survivors Tell Their Stories

Eating Disorder Survivors Tell Their Stories

Christina Chiu

The Rosen Publishing Group/New York

The Teen Health Library of Eating Disorder Prevention

Published in 1998 by the Rosen Publishing Group, Inc.
29 East 21st Street, New York, NY 10010

Library of Congress Cataloging-in-Publication Data

Chiu, Christina.
    Eating disorder survivors tell their stories / Christine Chiu. — 1st ed.
    p.cm. — (The teen health library of eating disorder prevention)
    Includes bibliographical references and index.
    Summary: Four survivors of anorexia nervosa, bulimia, and compulsive overeating share their experiences and give advice for the recovery of others.
    ISBN 0-8239-2767-9
    1. Eating disorders—Juvenile literature.   2. Anorexia nervosa—Juvenile literature.   3. Bulimia—Juvenile literature.   4. Body image—Juvenile literature.   5. Self-perception—Juvenile literature. [1. Anorexia nervosa. 2. Bulimia. 3. Eating disorders.] I. Title. II. Series.
RC552.E18C49 1998
616.85′26—dc21   98-4416
                                                                                              CIP
                                                                                               AC

Manufactured in the United States of America

Contents

Introduction

Food is essential to life. Food provides the nourishment our bodies need to function normally. But food is more than a substance we need in order to survive. It often provides comfort and joy. For example, certain foods sometimes have the ability to make a day seem brighter. Other foods may bring back memories of family gatherings or Thanksgiving dinners or other happy occasions.

But increasingly food has negative associations. It's common today for food to be associated with weight, fat, and diet. There are confusing mixed messages about food, health, and exercise. Many people no longer look at eating as an enjoyable practice that can bring people together. Instead many look at food and see only calories or fat. Some people stop eating foods they love altogether because they believe it will make them fat. Others force themselves to eat food they hate because it has less fat.

Our society encourages the idea that being thin is beautiful and sexy. And because of society's obsession

Many people find it hard to enjoy food. For them, food has negative associations with things such as weight, fat, and diet.

with weight and thinness, some people begin to think of food as an enemy.

Some people get stuck in a love-hate relationship with food or start hating it altogether. Do you or someone you know count calories when eating or feel you must exercise after eating to burn off the calories? Do you have a friend who diets excessively? Does he or she seem to go from diet to diet and seem to be losing too much weight? Do you know someone who "pigs out" and then disappears to the bathroom immediately after?

These are some of the signs that indicate that a person has or is in the process of developing an eating disorder. Eating disorders include anorexia nervosa, bulimia nervosa, and compulsive eating (also called binge-eating disorder). Millions of people in the United States suffer from one or more eating disorders. According to the National Association of Anorexia Nervosa and Associated Disorders (ANAD), as many as 7 million women and 1 million men suffer from eating disorders. They affect all kinds of people: young and old, rich and poor, as well as all minority groups. ANAD reports that on average, 90 percent of the sufferers are women and 10 percent are male. Recently the number of males with eating disorders has increased.

Most people find that their eating disorders started in their teenage years. Eighty-six percent report the onset of an eating disorder by age twenty. Forty-three percent report that the disorder started between ages sixteen and twenty. Especially alarming is that 10 percent of people with an eating disorder say it started as early as age ten or younger.

What Are Eating Disorders?

Anorexia Nervosa

People with anorexia nervosa intentionally starve themselves in an effort to lose weight. However, people suffering from this disorder are never satisfied with their weight loss. No matter how much weight they lose, they still believe they are overweight. This is dangerous because a person with anorexia does not get enough food to carry on normal functions. Vital organs, such as the heart, and bodily functions, such as a woman's ability to bear children, can be severely damaged over time.

Anorexia usually starts during the teen years, and the average victim falls at least 20 percent below his or her normal body weight. According to Becky Thompson, author of a book called *A Hunger So Wide and So Deep*, more than 1,000 women and girls die from anorexia every year.

Bulimia Nervosa

People suffering from bulimia will eat large amounts of food. They will then try to get rid of the excess calories by either inducing vomiting, abusing laxatives or diuretics, taking enemas, or exercising obsessively. This unhealthy behavior is known as bingeing and purging. These behaviors are often done in secret. A person with bulimia will often feel ashamed about his or her behavior and will try to keep it a secret from others. On the surface, it is difficult to tell if someone has bulimia, in part, because the person maintains a normal body weight.

Compulsive Eating

A similar disorder to bulimia is compulsive eating. People with bulimia eat excessive amounts and then purge, whereas compulsive eaters do not purge. People with this eating disorder lose control when they are bingeing. They stop eating only when their bodies are in physical pain. Many people who suffer from binge eating are overweight or obese.

What Causes Eating Disorders?

The causes of eating disorders are complex. Eating disorders often have more to do with control and boundary issues than with vanity or obsession with appearances. Eating disorders often are triggered by a combination of factors, such as problems at home, at school, or in relationships. These problems can cause difficult emotions, such as anger, hurt, and shame. But some teens don't know how to relieve the strong emotions and instead bottle them up. For teens who develop eating disorders, control of food becomes the outlet. A person may even suffer from more than one eating disorder at a time.

Eating Disorders and the Teen Years

The teen years are a time of change and growth. It is during this period that teens make the difficult transition from child to adult. This time of life is often very stressful and is marked by changes in the physical body, emotions, and thoughts.

Because of these changes, some teens feel as if they are losing control over their bodies and lives. To maintain that sense of control in their lives, some teens turn to controlling food. Some of the teens in this book talk about using their eating disorder as a way to gain some control over their lives. They also use their eating disorders to express emotions and anger that they couldn't otherwise release.

People who eat compulsively or have bulimia binge—they eat huge amounts of food in one sitting. Those with bulimia then purge their bodies of the food by inducing vomiting, taking enemas, abusing laxatives, or exercising compulsively.

Consequences of Eating Disorders

The results of eating disorders can be physically harmful. For instance, teens suffering from anorexia risk starving themselves to death. This disease can cause serious, irreparable damage to vital organs, such as the heart and brain. Patients with bulimia can cause damage to their esophagus and stomach from excessive vomiting. Stomach acids brought up through vomiting can also wear away the protective coating on teeth. Binge eaters tend to be overweight and are at risk of high cholesterol, high blood pressure, and diabetes.

Besides the physical dangers, eating disorders can cause great emotional damage. ANAD reports that victims can often suffer from severe depression, feelings of shame and guilt, low self-esteem, and withdrawal. As a result, sufferers can have difficulty maintaining relationships with family, friends, and coworkers.

In this book, you will read about the struggles of four young people who have battled with eating disorders. These teens talk about their experiences with anorexia, bulimia, and compulsive eating, and how they dealt with these disorders. Hopefully their experiences will help you or someone you know overcome an eating disorder or prevent one from developing. Some people fully recover from their eating disorders. For others it is a lifelong struggle, but with time it gets easier. The most important thing is that you recognize you have a problem and you work toward regaining control of your life.

If you or someone you know has an eating disorder, it is important to reach out and get help. You may feel that your eating disorder is taking over your life, but it doesn't have to control you. Eating disorders can be treated. You don't have to be a slave to them. You can take back control of your life. You can be happy with yourself and your body.

Barbara: Compulsive Eating

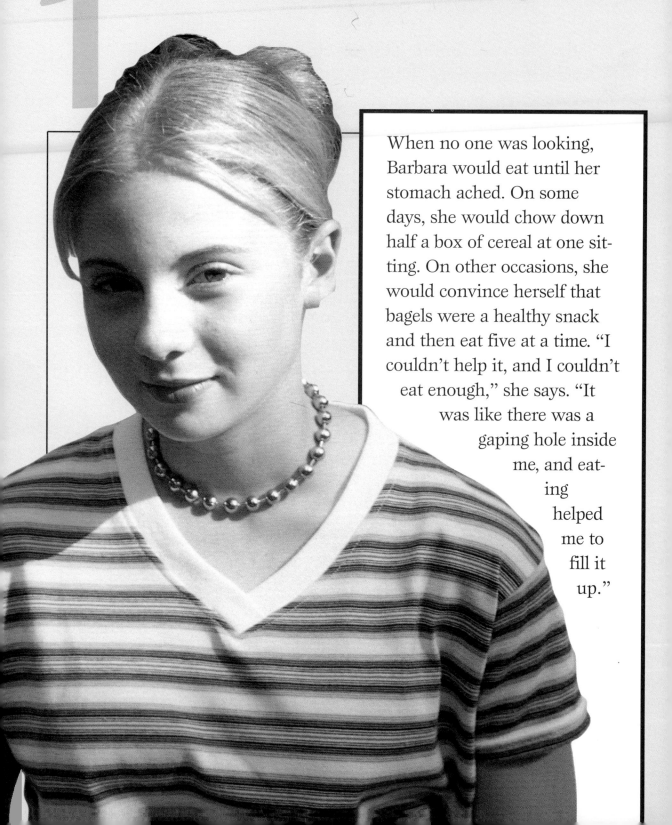

When no one was looking, Barbara would eat until her stomach ached. On some days, she would chow down half a box of cereal at one sitting. On other occasions, she would convince herself that bagels were a healthy snack and then eat five at a time. "I couldn't help it, and I couldn't eat enough," she says. "It was like there was a gaping hole inside me, and eating helped me to fill it up."

Even though bingeing made her physically sick, she was determined to continue. "I'm going to fill this space with however much it takes," she told herself.

Barbara doesn't remember when her eating got out of control, but when she turned seventeen, she suddenly gained twenty-five pounds within a four-month period. "My clothes didn't fit," she says. "I'd ask myself, 'What's going on?'" Her weight became a major issue at home. Her parents told her, "We're not going to buy more clothes for you." They even blamed her for being overweight, arguing that she needed to exercise more self-control.

Barbara tried but couldn't control her eating habits, often bingeing in secret even though it made her feel guilty and horrible. "In front of my parents, I ate what they thought I should eat, even though I was already totally stuffed," she says. "I didn't want them to know."

Barbara says these binges were like "missions." Although her parents told her eating was a matter of self-control, for Barbara, it was more than that. Her compulsive eating was an instant way to numb painful emotions and feelings of loneliness. Socially, it felt as if her life were crumbling around her. Once athletic, Barbara was no longer participating in any sport. Her close friend at school dumped her to hang out with the popular crowd. She was close to her brother, but he was away at college. Suddenly, she

Sometimes it is hard to admit that you may be developing an eating disorder. Talking to your parents or someone else you trust about your problems with food can help.

felt as though she had no companionship, no one with whom to share her problems. "I felt really lonely all of a sudden," she says. "I was miserable." Bingeing became her way to dull her feelings of loneliness and sadness.

Her parents stressed that she had to lose weight. At dinner, even when guests were present, her parents offered dessert to everyone at the table except Barbara. "It was demoralizing," Barbara says. She resented her parents' behavior because it seemed as if they were trying to tell her that losing weight or being skinny would somehow make her a better person. It was as if being heavy meant she wasn't good enough—that she was a bad person.

Barbara went through a roller-coaster ride of excessive dieting and then excessive bingeing. Before she left for college, she started exercising and eating better, losing the weight she had gained. But once in college, she reverted back to her unhealthy eating habits. The stresses of a new school and a different social environment drove Barbara to start bingeing once again.

While home for the summer break during her junior year, her parents sat her down for a talk. They said, "There's a problem. You're really secretive about this, but we know you must be eating in between meals when we aren't around." Again, they emphasized the importance of losing weight. "Up until that point, I thought [my problem with binge eating] would go away," Barbara says. "But I could not stop. I finally accepted that I had a problem and that I needed help."

The next day, Barbara went to an eating disorders unit for an assessment of her eating problem. The doctors admitted her into their outpatient program. As part of the recovery process, Barbara attended therapy sessions at the eating disorders unit. In therapy, she came to realize that she was really angry with her parents. She didn't want to be. She knew they had good intentions and meant to help her, but still she felt bitter that they refused to see that she was suffering from a serious emotional

Most people suffering from eating disorders try to hide their problems with food from their family and friends.

problem. Despite her parents' good intentions, Barbara felt their message to her was, "You need to control yourself better."

The clinic helped Barbara confront painful experiences from her past as well as learn how to deal with difficult feelings in healthier ways. She found that her compulsive eating habits were rooted in her childhood. Barbara remembered that on her tenth birthday, her mother had baked a huge birthday cake. She became obsessed with sneaking the leftovers of the cake. "I had to eat it," she says. "I was not a fat kid, but I tried to cut [the cake] so no one would know I was doing it." Barbara knew that if her mother found out, she would have said eating more than one piece was piggish and overly indulgent. Yet Barbara could not stop making secret trips to the refrigerator.

Therapy brought up painful memories about Barbara's weight. These memories came from the time she was seven. "Mom put me on a diet," she says. "I was chubby—not fat—and I couldn't bring dessert to camp with my lunch. I was the only kid with no dessert—everyone else had fun things. In my head, I was the fat kid who couldn't have things that other kids have."

Denial of her problems became a big part of her compulsive eating habits. "I felt deprived," she says. "Then, when I binged, I felt I couldn't eat enough. My instinct was that I shouldn't be eating full meals," she says. "I would go from depriving myself to feeling as though I was deserving of all those calories." At the eating disorders unit, Barbara was forced to eat regular meals. The goal at the unit was for her not to deprive herself of food. "They helped me recognize that if I ate normally, it would help me stop bingeing."

As a result of therapy, Barbara also learned a lot about her parents. Her father joined her in family therapy but refused to acknowledge that Barbara was suffering from a serious emotional problem. "Dad was in complete denial. He couldn't accept any responsibility of doing anything wrong," she

Many of our beliefs about food and eating come from our parents and other family members. Sometimes these ideas can be unhealthy.

says. "He was big on self-control. He had been chubby in his thirties, and after deciding fats and sweets were 'poison,' he stopped eating them and managed to lose the weight."

Her mother believed that Barbara was beautiful, but always insisted that Barbara should get down to a size eight. While at the eating disorders clinic,

Barbara finally realized that her mother's goal was not only unrealistic and unhealthy but would be impossible to achieve. Good health depends on following a balanced diet and getting the proper amount of exercise. No chart can tell you how much you should weigh or what clothing size you should wear. Each person's body is different.

Barbara came to understand her relationship with food. Though she was constantly trying to lose weight, another part of her refused to give her parents what they wanted—her weight loss. "Food kept me from certain kinds of emotional stress, but it was also a kind of protective shield," she says. "It was safety and comfort."

These days, Barbara has gained control of her eating habits, but she still struggles with mini-relapses. However, the binges have gradually become less extreme. "I'm finally accepting that it's a lifelong process," she says. "But at least now, when I struggle with it, I have the tools that I've learned for fighting the urge to eat compulsively," she says. When she feels the urge to eat, she steps back and asks herself, "Am I hungry or should I write in my journal?"

Barbara's Advice

Barbara believes that many factors in her life helped her recover from her eating disorder. She advises young people with similar problems to reach out and find supportive people who can help them. Barbara says therapy has played an important role in her recovery. "When I need to, I meet with a therapist every week. It helps to talk about stuff going on in my life."

Barbara also keeps a journal of her thoughts. "Writing every few days keeps me in touch with what's going on inside. When I feel like eating compulsively, it's important to stop and figure out what's really going on." When you can't speak with someone or there is no one you feel you can talk to, write down

When you feel an urge to eat compulsively, writing down your thoughts and feelings may help you control it. Keeping a journal may also help you better understand and cope with your emotions.

your thoughts. Jotting down your thoughts can help you understand them better and deal with them.

Barbara suggests keeping busy with activities that will occupy you so that you don't think about food. "I'll do things that are fun and I like. It's important to keep myself occupied until that feeling goes away. I'll listen to music or go for a jog."

And lastly, Barbara suggests calling friends. "It's important to have contact with friends. Reach out. Your friends will be there for you and help you to feel less lonely."

Gary: Anorexia Nervosa and Compulsive Exercise

2

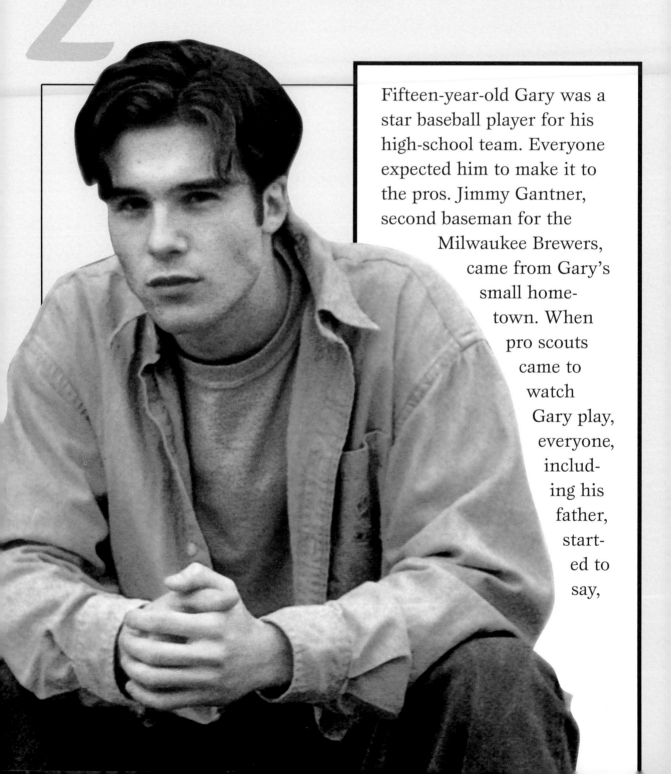

Fifteen-year-old Gary was a star baseball player for his high-school team. Everyone expected him to make it to the pros. Jimmy Gantner, second baseman for the Milwaukee Brewers, came from Gary's small home-town. When pro scouts came to watch Gary play, everyone, includ-ing his father, start-ed to say,

"Gary's going to be the next Jimmy Gantner." "I loved baseball," Gary says, "but I didn't want to play at such a competitive level—it was too much pressure." He never told anyone how he really felt. "I thought they'd think I was nuts and they'd reject me," he says, "especially my father."

But because of the pressure Gary felt, he started training the way the pros train. He exercised alone two hours before school, then again after school with the baseball team. At home, after dinner, he would exercise for another two hours. "It became an obsession," Gary says. He couldn't control what people thought of or expected from him. He could not control his fear of rejection. "These workouts were the only way I knew how to control and deal with the pressure." Gary began exercising compulsively, which is an eating disorder–related behavior.

The workouts were excessive, but what really triggered Gary's anorexia was his denial of food. At first his diet started out healthy. He ate nutritious, well-balanced meals three times a day, cutting down on fatty foods. But then he cut out all fatty foods and stopped eating desserts altogether. "I loved desserts but it was part of the denial," he explains. "In a way, I didn't feel I deserved them."

His problem with food took firm hold when he started to eat less food, cutting his daily calories from 2,000 to 1,500 to 1,000 to 500—while sticking to his rigorous workouts. His weight dropped rapidly. When his mother questioned him about it, Gary used baseball as an excuse. He tried to convince her that this was how he needed to train to make it in the pros. Gary is 5′7″ with a medium to large bone structure. A healthy weight for Gary would have been between 145 to 160 pounds. At the peak of his anorexia, Gary weighed 104 pounds.

"I thought about food all day and all night," he says. "I was obsessed with my weight and calories and told myself I had to get [my weight] lower and then even lower." He became obsessive about working out every day at exactly the same time, doing one hundred sit-ups every morning. It became his prime focus.

The obsession with weight and calories became his way to cope with life, pressure, low self-esteem, and the anger he was trying to bury. "[Control] was my best friend," he says. "There were times when my parents put half a glass of milk—just a few gulps—in front of me, demanding that I drink it. But I refused. I wouldn't let them take my best friend—the control—away from me." He saw control over food as power. He took pride in starving himself. "Being hungry meant success. It meant I was beating the hunger," he says. "It was painful, but it felt comfortable, because I was in control."

Worried by Gary's behavior, his mother discussed the situation with a close friend, describing her

Many teens feel pressured by their parents to excel in activities such as school and sports. For these teens, obsessively controlling their weight helps them to feel as if they have control over their lives.

son's workouts and eating patterns. The woman confirmed that Gary might have an eating disorder. A couple of days later, Gary's mother made an appointment for an evaluation at an eating disorders clinic. Gary was diagnosed with anorexia nervosa and was admitted as an inpatient to the hospital.

When Gary was admitted to the hospital, his father put his arms around Gary, trying to hug him. "I love you and want what's best for you," he said.

Gary didn't even acknowledge his father. "I felt nothing—no feelings of remorse, no guilt. I just wanted to get those sit-ups done."

As a result of anorexia, Gary had lost close to forty pounds. He had no body fat left, and his body was starting to burn muscle tissue. His blood pressure was so low that he passed out frequently. But even then, he felt he hadn't lost enough weight. His goal was to get down to ninety-five pounds. "When I told my psychiatrist at the hospital, he looked at me and said, 'I have to be honest with you. You're so malnourished that if you get down to ninety-five pounds, you will have only three weeks to a month to live.'" At the time, Gary wasn't scared of death. His condition was so severe that not enough glucose was going to his brain. "I felt numb, like I was on drugs," he says. "My feelings of anger, fear, and sadness were numbed, too."

The staff at the eating disorders unit put Gary on a strict food plan, forcing him to eat regular meals. The hospital team threatened to feed him intravenously (IV) if he didn't eat 2,000 calories a day. Opting for food over an IV, he ate three meals every day. A nurse sat with him while he ate every bite. He had to sit for an hour after every meal to make sure the food was digested. Gary would then secretly try to work off the meal.

Looking back, Gary now realizes that part of the problem was communication. "Not being able to express my feelings made me angry, and I turned

Some teens develop eating disorders as a way to release their emotions. To recover, they have to work with their families to create a healthy environment in which it's okay to express feelings such as fear, anger, and unhappiness.

that anger on myself," he says. Gary had a very loving family, but one that didn't express "bad" emotions. Conflict was forbidden. Feelings such as anger, pain, or sadness were not okay. Everything had to be good. Everyone had to be happy. He felt that he had to walk around with a "happy face" regardless of how terrible he might be feeling inside. At the dinner table, the family never talked about world issues, since people might have differing opinions, which might spark arguments.

"If a person stuffs [his or her emotion], it's going to come out somehow," Gary says. "I was angry because it wasn't okay to say, 'I don't want to do this instead of that,' and I felt the responsibility to please people all the time." All the pressure built up inside him, and because he couldn't express what he really wished—to just play baseball for fun and nothing else—he ended up taking it out on himself. "I hated myself," he says. "I never made plans to commit suicide or even considered it, but I wanted to die, and this was the way—painful and slow—I was trying to do it."

Gary was in and out of the hospital for the next seven years. The disease took a toll on both his physical and psychological well-being. It isolated him from friends and family. Not only did Gary drop out of the school baseball team, but he was forced to retake his senior year of high school. "Over time, [the eating disorder] took over my entire life," he says.

Eventually Gary started to see a therapist trained in eating disorders. He

A healthy, balanced diet is important for both your physical and psychological well-being.

Therapy can help you recognize feelings, such as fear and anger, and deal with them in a positive way.

also took part in group therapy with other eating disordered people. Step by step, he confronted his feelings and learned how to deal with his anger. Even more important, he learned how to relinquish control, which was at the heart of his eating problem. His family was supportive and went through counseling with him, too. "It was the first time that I told my dad that I loved him but I didn't want to play baseball at a competitive level," he says. "We never talked like this or did these kinds of things before."

During his last visit, the doctors at the hospital told him, "You've gotten all the counseling that we feel you need, and you know everything you need to know. We have confidence that you'll be able to

You cannot recover from an eating disorder all at once. It takes time and patience. But, remember, you *can* get better.

let this go." Because the hospital staff showed Gary that they were responsible to him and not for him, Gary realized for the first time that he had to be responsible for himself. He had to decide if he wanted to hang on to his eating disorder for the rest of his life or not. It was up to him. He had to do the work.

"It hit me how much energy it took to hold on to it," he says. "I asked myself if it was worth it anymore." He finally decided, "No more."

Gary's Advice

Gary believes counseling is a great tool in the recovery

process from anorexia. "Counseling helped me understand and look at my issues of low self-esteem." Gary also believes teens should see a registered dietitian to learn the proper ways to eat healthy, well-balanced meals.

Recovering from anorexia is not something that can be done all at once. Gary suggests creating a week-by-week strategy. "I didn't just stop exercising. I cut back little by little." Don't try to do everything all at once. It takes time and patience. Many people battle with the disease for many years.

Gary suggests getting involved in other activities. "Whenever I'd get the craving to exercise, I'd go elsewhere—to a different room or out of the house altogether. The important thing was to get my mind off of it. I'd read a book or watch television or go out with a friend." Although religion may not be for everyone, Gary says, "There's a certain security in religion that I haven't found elsewhere."

It's important to get support from people in your life, such as your family, your friends, and your doctors. "When I needed support, I turned to my parents and other patients and nurses that I met at the hospital," Gary says.

Pilar: Bulimia

3

Being a biracial child of African American and Latin parents made seventeen-year-old Pilar's life especially difficult when her family moved into an all-white community.

"There was a lot of name-calling from the other kids," she says. "Because of stereotypes, teachers thought Latinos weren't smart people, and they expected me to do poorly." As a result, Pilar felt she had to work harder, trying to maintain an A average in all her classes. "If I got a B on a test, I'd be like, 'Oh, God, they're right.' I'd feel outnumbered and powerless. I'd give up." When boys at school teased Pilar and called her ugly, she ended up getting in fistfights—and was sometimes sent home from school.

When Pilar tried to tell her parents what was happening in school, they scolded her. "They didn't want to hear it," she says. "They'd say, 'We worked so hard to get here. You're so lucky. You have privileges that we didn't have.'"

Pilar's parents told her that she shouldn't be distracted by people like that. They told her, "You're above that."

"I was the only person in the family trying to be honest about my experience," she says. "But then they'd say, 'You're so ungrateful.'"

Pilar's weight has always been an issue in her family. Her parents had always told her she needed to lose weight. They put Pilar on her first diet—500 calories per day—when she was only in the third grade. Looking back, she now realizes, "I wasn't overweight. I was just taller and more developed, but they didn't see that," she says. "They wanted me to have a lanky body, but I just didn't have that kind of body type."

Being in a new neighborhood and in a school with hostile students greatly hurt Pilar's self-esteem. She

Everyone wants to be accepted by other people. Society often tells us that to be popular, successful, and happy, we have to be thin.

didn't want others to think she was ugly—she wanted to be accepted by them.

Because of all the pressures she was facing, Pilar used food for comfort. Food became a way to soothe herself. Whenever she was upset, Pilar turned to the food for comfort, often gorging herself and then forcing herself to throw up. The idea for purging came to her from a book she read about a ballerina who ate and then threw it up. The story included vivid descriptions of the dancer purging her food.

"I would eat my anger away—push it down with food," Pilar remembers. "Then I'd purge it by throwing up. The act was almost violent, and it seemed like victory."

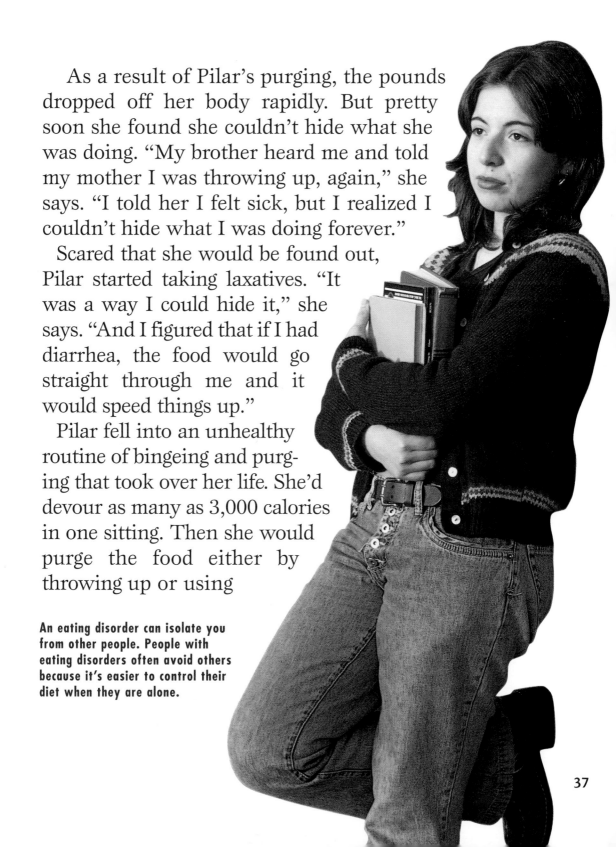

As a result of Pilar's purging, the pounds dropped off her body rapidly. But pretty soon she found she couldn't hide what she was doing. "My brother heard me and told my mother I was throwing up, again," she says. "I told her I felt sick, but I realized I couldn't hide what I was doing forever."

Scared that she would be found out, Pilar started taking laxatives. "It was a way I could hide it," she says. "And I figured that if I had diarrhea, the food would go straight through me and it would speed things up."

Pilar fell into an unhealthy routine of bingeing and purging that took over her life. She'd devour as many as 3,000 calories in one sitting. Then she would purge the food either by throwing up or using

An eating disorder can isolate you from other people. People with eating disorders often avoid others because it's easier to control their diet when they are alone.

laxatives. "I couldn't go anywhere," she says. "I never ate in public, only at home. Everything was planned out, like what food I would eat. I was afraid if I ate when I went out with friends, there would not be a bathroom I could use that was private. I had no social life."

At the height of the bulimia, Pilar says that her relationship with food became like an addiction. "There was no room for anything else," she says, "even my emotions." All of Pilar's energy and attention were focused on food.

Pilar would binge for weeks, eating excessive amounts of food, which would result in large weight gain. Then she would start purging everything she ate until she reached the "right" size. "It was totally clothing and scale driven," she says, "I was 5'6", and I would purge until I was 140 pounds and able to wear a size ten."

Once she reached that goal, she would start eating compulsively again. "I was so out of touch with my body that all of a sudden I couldn't wear my clothes anymore," she says. "I'd wake up one day, and I'd be in a panic, like, 'Oh, no.'"

Pilar continued bingeing and purging. When she was eighteen, she realized she was in trouble when her body automatically purged something she ate even though she hadn't intended to throw it up. She told herself she had to stop. "I thought it was

Teens with eating disorders often believe that losing weight will make them more attractive and popular. Instead, they find it very difficult to live a normal life and to interact with other people.

a matter of self-control," Pilar says. But the bulimia had taken over. No matter how much she wanted to eat normally and lead a normal life, she found that she could not stop. Her bulimia prevented her from participating in normal social activities. As a result, she became increasingly depressed and isolated.

"In my mind, I started purging to lose weight so that I would be more attractive and, as a result, be more popular and worthy of others' interaction," Pilar says. "But what resulted was that I wasn't able to interact at all. It became impossible to keep this 'secret' and be with people at the same time."

Pilar knew she needed help and went to see a therapist. However, the experience was disastrous. Pilar says her therapist was uninformed and inexperienced. The therapist told Pilar that she did not have a problem and did not need help. Discouraged, Pilar gave up on therapy.

It wasn't until she was nineteen, when things felt as if they were falling apart and her grades started to slip dramatically, that Pilar willingly tried therapy again. "My eating disorder was an issue of control," she says. "But I reached the point where I couldn't function. I realized I was out of control, and this propelled me to get help."

This time, Pilar found a place where people were able and willing to help her. In therapy, she dealt with the underlying issues, which became essential to her recovery process from bulimia. "I needed to deal with my emotions," she says. "I didn't realize this until later, but emotionally I was really immature, and in a way, my e.d. [eating disorder] was self-medicating. I had been emotionally vacant." Finally facing and learning to deal with her emotions made Pilar see her life in a totally new way. "I realized I didn't want to live that way anymore," she says.

Food issues are still a day-to-day struggle for Pilar. She says, "When I'm under a lot of stress, I still feel like purging, and I want to lose weight." But today Pilar has learned to keep her urges in check. Although she no longer binges and purges, the long-term aftereffects have been devastating to her body. As a result of her eating disorder, Pilar stopped menstruating when she was seventeen.

Every bodily function takes energy, but when the body isn't receiving enough energy to carry on its normal functions, the body will protect itself. To preserve energy, the body will shut off functions, such as menstruation, that aren't necessary for the body to survive. Since Pilar's body didn't have the energy to sustain the reproductive process, her body shut off that function.

Though Pilar started to recover from bulimia when she was twenty and her period started again, she developed a condition called chronic uterine cystitis. This condition is the direct result of Pilar's purging and starving her body during her teen years when her body was still growing and developing. The condition causes recurring cysts to develop in the uterus. As a result, Pilar may not ever be able to have children.

"I thought [my problems] were over when the bulimia stopped," she says. "But now I have to live with this every day, and it's hard. It's a reminder that, no matter what, I can't go back [to suffering from bulimia and hurting herself]."

Pilar's Advice

Pilar believes therapy can greatly help in the recovery process, if you can find the right people. "Private therapy helped me to understand my relationship to food. It helped me deal with the emotions that caused the eating disorder," says Pilar.

Pilar also recommends yoga and meditation. "Yoga helped me to focus on myself in a way that allowed the anxieties to lessen. It made me feel centered and taught me how to

There are productive ways to deal with stress and emotions. Activities such as yoga, meditation, and relaxation exercises can help to relieve the pressures of everyday life.

42

focus on each moment. I had to tell myself, 'One thing at a time,' " Pilar says. "Before, I'd compound all my stresses and problems and it would make me feel doomed. But now I can slow myself down. Instead of letting things happen to me, I'll ask what I can do to change this. From there, I'll plan a strategic attack."

Pilar suggests that those who are avoiding their emotions or using their control of food as a way to deal with feelings should face their emotions. "I try to be conscious about what I'm feeling and what I'm eating. Instead of letting my emotions go underground, I try to deal with them as they arise," says Pilar. When she feels like bingeing, she stops and asks herself why she is doing this and what is making her feel that way. "Usually, I'll get an answer that relates more directly than the cookies or a bag of chips," says Pilar.

Nicole: Bulimia

Nicole, seventeen, felt all kinds of pressures from the people in her life. Her Chinese parents expected her to get straight As and to get into a good college. Her friends wanted her to hang out even when she had to study for a big test the next day.

Her new boyfriend pressured her to have sex. Although she had expectations for herself, Nicole wanted to please everyone. She wanted to be smart, cool, and mature enough to do the things that she knew she wasn't ready for. She wanted to dress right, look right, and say all the right things.

At times, being a Chinese American further complicated things. "If I did something wrong," she says, "I was always afraid people would think, 'Hey, all Chinese people do that.' Sounds silly, but I felt all this pressure to do things right."

Nicole says food became a major issue in her life when she joined her school's gymnastics team. "That first week of practice, a lot of the girls had aching wrists or knees. The coach sat us down to say, 'There's a lot of pounding in this sport. Some of you—and you know who you are—have excess baggage that you're throwing around, and it isn't going to help those sore joints you've got.' "

Nicole says she didn't think she was overweight but, like all her friends on the team, she started to become extremely aware of all the foods she ate. "During meets, it's impossible to hide anything when you're wearing only a leotard," she says. She became critically conscious of her appearance.

The bulimia seemed to creep up on Nicole. She can't remember the first time she forced herself to throw up. Looking back, she says, "I used to get so tense and

nervous—it made me sick to my stomach. Throwing up didn't seem like a problem because I thought I was always on the verge of a cold or flu."

But her obsession with bingeing and purging started to get worse. "The more I told myself I could not eat, the more I had to eat. When no one was around, I would [eat] all kinds of junk—bags of candy, boxes of doughnuts, leftovers from dinner, ice cream—until I really did feel sick. Then I'd make a beeline for the bathroom and throw it all up," she says. "Sometimes I'd eat a big dinner with my parents and then purge that, too."

Secrecy about her bulimia became a powerful

People suffering from eating disorders often try desperately to hide their disease from their family and friends. Unfortunately, this secrecy prevents them from getting the help they need.

obsession. Nicole says, "When I was stuck in a situation when I couldn't throw up—other people were around or I was in a place where people would hear me—I would freak out. Not on the outside, but on the inside. A part of me would imagine the food I just ate turning into fat. I'd panic until I figured a way to get out of there."

Hostage to her eating disorder, Nicole started to adjust her schedule around her eating habits. "I stopped going anyplace I wasn't certain I'd be able to use a bathroom in private," she says. The result was that Nicole didn't go out much. "I wanted to hang out with friends, but I couldn't," she says. "The bulimia came first, before anything."

Even though she started vomiting meals as often as twice a day, Nicole didn't realize how her eating disorder was affecting her body. "It wasn't until my yearly visit to the dentist that I realized things weren't normal," she says. Nicole didn't realize that the stomach acid from her vomit had eaten away parts of her tooth enamel and had caused ridges in her teeth.

"My dentist didn't come right out and say anything. What he said was, 'It seems that you have a few ridges along the front of your teeth.' I said, 'Really?' as if I didn't know what he meant. But he looked at me weird, then handed me a mirror. The edge of my front teeth was noticeably jagged. He

If you fear you have an eating disorder, you can turn to a friend, family member, school counselor or nurse, coach, or teacher. You can also call one of the organizations listed in the back of this book for help.

asked if I wanted him to file my teeth smooth."

"Of course I said yes," says Nicole. "After I left his office, I knew if I kept throwing up like that, my teeth would get those ridges again, and my dentist would know for sure."

She decided she had to stop. Nicole went to talk with the school nurse, who was already a trusted friend. "She let me talk," Nicole says. "She also got me this book about eating disorders and arranged for me to meet with the school psychologist."

Meeting the school psychologist was difficult because Nicole wanted to keep her eating disorder a secret from friends. "It was scary," she says. "When I was purging, I'd always be afraid that someone would hear me in the stall or something. When I started seeing the school psychologist, I was afraid people would notice and somehow know about me."

Luckily, Nicole finally told her best friend Jane. "I thought she'd freak out, but she was really cool about it. She didn't pretend to know what it was like, and she didn't constantly ask me if I was okay. She treated me normal."

The school psychologist gave Nicole the tools she needed to deal with the pressures of school, peers, and family. "Talking things out really helped. I learned how to express my feelings and emotions to other people instead of taking it out on myself. Therapy helped me realize that I was using the bulimia as a sort of crutch, and that falling back on it would only make things worse." The school psychologist also gave Nicole books to read about bulimia, which gave Nicole a better understanding about the disease.

Learning how to deal with the different kinds of pressures in her life as well as the people who contributed to her stress was the first major step in Nicole's recovery process. "Instead of throwing up every time something bad happened, I had to deal

Learning how to deal with the pressures of life is often the first step in recovering from an eating disorder.

with it," remembers Nicole. "But it forced me to say to my boyfriend, 'I love you, and I don't want to lose you, but I'm not ready for sex.' It forced me to say to my parents, 'I want to go to a good college, too, but I need you to stop pressuring me about my grades so much.' "

Recovery from bulimia isn't easy. "There are times even now—five years later—that I find myself in a food panic. But now, whenever I feel the urge to chow and purge an entire cake, I stop myself and ask, 'Why? Am I really hungry? Or is it because I'm anxious or feeling pressured by something else?' "

Every time Nicole makes it through this kind of panic, she feels all the more confident. "Now I know I'm in charge. Every time I beat that feeling, it's like saying, 'This is my body and my life.' "

Nicole's Advice

Like the others in this book, Nicole believes that speaking with either a psychologist or a trained eating disorder professional is very important in the recovery process. When Nicole feels the urge to throw up, she goes for a walk to clear her thoughts. "Think about why you want to throw up. Is it that you are sick or is it that you're feeling anxious about something else?"

Nicole also suggests talking to others about what's on your mind. "If you're upset with someone, talk to him or her about it. If that isn't possible, at least speak with a psychologist." There are also many eating disorder groups on-line with whom you can share your experiences.

Eating Disorders: A Cry for Help

5

You have just read the stories of four young people and their battles with and recovery process from eating disorders. Each of the stories is different, but they also share similar themes. Being a teenager is sometimes difficult. You face pressures from your parents, friends, and school. But if you are using your control of food as a way to cope with your problems, hopefully this book has shown you the destructive consequences of such a coping method. There are healthier ways to cope.

All of the young people interviewed in this book used eating disorders as a way to deal with their feelings. Some said their disorders became their way to cope with life and to numb feelings of anger or sadness. Others say that the obsession with food took every ounce of their energy and helped them to avoid the real issues that were bothering them. They saw food as the only aspect in their lives that they could control.

There's a cost for trying to achieve that kind of control. Anorexia alone claims more than 1,000 lives each year. In addition to the serious physical damage that they can cause, eating disorders can also cause emotional pain to the sufferers, their families, and friends.

Eating disorders are a cry for help. People who develop eating disorders often use the condition to express or release emotions or desires that they don't know how to deal with. Everyone feels powerless and overwhelmed by his or her emotions from time to time. If you sometimes feel this way too, there's nothing wrong with you. However, if you think that you cannot cope with your emotions and the pressures of daily life, it may be time to get help.

By reaching out for help early, you may be able to prevent developing an eating disorder by learning more effective ways to cope with stress.

If you think you may already be suffering from an eating disorder, it is not too late for you. The experiences of the teens in this book prove that no one is ever beyond help. Perhaps you know that you suffer from anorexia nervosa, bulimia nervosa, compulsive eating, or compulsive exercise, but you do not know what to do.

The first step is to talk to someone. You may want to turn to a parent, a sibling, or another trusted relative. Perhaps a teacher, guidance counselor, school psychologist, or coach can help. You also can ask your friends to assist you. If you do not know anyone that you feel comfortable telling about your eating disorder, you may want to call one of the numbers listed at the back of this book. Many are free and anonymous. You can speak to a trained eating disorder counselor without having to give him or her your name.

Once you have decided you need help and have found someone who will support you, you may want to consider entering therapy. The teens in this book who struggled with their eating disorders say that therapy—whether one-on-one with a psychologist or with a group—makes a tremendous difference. Therapy can help you deal with your emotions. It also will show you that, as a victim of an eating disorder, you are not alone. Many teens are currently struggling with the same issues that you are. You can support one another. You can learn from others' mistakes as well as their successes.

Many people suffering from eating disorders claim that inpatient or outpatient hospitalization saved their lives because they were forced to deal with the real source of their diseases—the pain inside them. Depending upon the severity of your disease, inpatient or outpatient treatment may help you. A counselor can talk with you and your parents to help decide what type of treatment is best for you. Inpatient, outpatient, and structured therapy treatments are all effective ways to overcome an eating disorder.

Survivors say that part of their eating disorders will always be in their lives. Although they may have recovered, the obsessive feelings that caused their eating disorders show up again from time to time. This is especially true in times of stress.

However, survivors also say that they have confronted and beaten their eating disorders—they have survived. Although they may occasionally have obsessive thoughts about food, they are able to live normal lives. Obsessions with eating and food have not taken over their lives. Many eating disorder survivors are happy, productive, and successful individuals. They are also wiser because of the struggles they have experienced.

Eating disorder survivors have learned more effective and constructive ways to cope with their problems. Relearning methods to cope with emotional stress—whether writing daily in a journal or going for a long walk—is crucial to recovery. Rather than internalizing and suppressing their feelings, survivors look for ways to express and release them.

Glossary

anorexia nervosa An eating disorder in which one intentionally starves oneself.

binge To consume large amounts of food, often in secret and usually without control.

bulimia nervosa An eating disorder in which a person eats normal or large amounts of food and then rids the body of the food by either forcing oneself to vomit, abusing laxatives or diuretics, taking enemas, or exercising obsessively.

calorie A unit to measure the energy-producing value of food.

compulsive eating An eating disorder marked by uncontrollable eating of large amounts of food.

demoralize To bring down someone's morale or self-esteem.

denial Refusing to admit or face the truth or reality of a situation.

depression A state of extreme and prolonged sadness.

deprive To withhold something from or take something away.

indulgent Giving in easily to wants and desires.

inpatient A patient who remains in a hospital or a clinic for treatment.

internalize To bottle up problems or emotions.

obsessive Excessive to the point of being unreasonable.

outpatient A patient in a clinic or hospital who does not live in the hospital but visits on a regular basis for treatment.

overachiever A person who strives for success beyond what is expected.

psychiatrist A doctor who is trained to treat people with mental, emotional, or behavioral disorders.

ravenous A state of extreme hunger.

self-esteem Confidence or satisfaction in oneself; self-respect.

Where to Go for Help

American Anorexia/Bulimia Association, Inc. (AABA)
165 West 46th Street, #1108
New York, NY 10036
(212) 575-6200
Web site: http://members.aol.com/AMANBU

Anorexia Nervosa and Related Eating Disorders, Inc. (ANRED)
Box 5102
Eugene, OR 97405
(541) 344-1144
Web site: http://www.anred.com

Eating Disorders Awareness and Prevention, Inc. (EDAP)
603 Stewart Street, Suite 803
Seattle, WA 98101
(206) 382-3587
Web site: http://members.aol.com/edapinc

National Association of Anorexia Nervosa and Associated Disorders, Inc. (ANAD)
Box 7
Highland Park, IL 60035
(847) 831-3438
Web site: http://www.members.aol.com/anad20/index.html

National Eating Disorders Organization (NEDO)
6655 South Yale Avenue
Tulsa, OK 74136
(918) 481-4044
Web site: http://www.laureate.com

Overeaters Anonymous
P. O. Box 44020
Rio Rancho, NM 87174
(505) 891-2664
Web site: http://www.overeatersanonymous.org

In Canada

The National Eating Disorder Information Centre
College Wing, 1st Floor, Room 211
200 Elizabeth Street
Toronto, ON M5G 2C4
(416) 340-4156

For Further Reading

Boskind-White, Marlene, and William C. White. *Bulimarexia: The Binge/Purge Cycle.* New York: W. W. Norton & Co., 1991.

Chernin, Kim. *The Hungry Self: Women, Eating, and Identity.* New York: HarperPerennial, 1994.

Hornbacher, Marya. *Wasted: A Memoir of Anorexia and Bulimia.* New York: HarperCollins, 1998.

Jantz, Gregory L. *Hope, Help, and Healing for Eating Disorders.* Wheaton, Ill.: Harold Shaw Publishers, 1995.

Kolodny, Nancy J. *When Food's a Foe: How You Can Confront and Conquer Your Eating Disorder.* Boston: Little Brown, 1992.

Orenstein, Peggy. *SchoolGirls.* New York: Anchor Books, 1994.

Pipher, Mary. *Hunger Pains: The Modern Woman's Tragic Quest for Thinness.* New York: Ballantine Books, 1995.

Roth, Geneen. *Feeding the Hungry Heart: The Experience of Compulsive Eating.* New York: Plume, 1993.

Sheppard, Kay. *Food Addiction: The Body Knows.* Deerfield Beach, Fla.: Health Communications, 1993.

Siegal, Michele, Judith Brisman, and Margot Weinshel. *Surviving an Eating Disorder: Strategies for Family and Friends.* New York: HarperPerennial, 1997.

Index

About the Author

Christina Chiu is a freelance writer in New York City. She was a writer and editor at the Children's Television Workshop and Scholastic, Inc. She also worked on a teen Web site at *Parade Magazine*. Currently, Ms. Chiu is receiving her M.F.A. in creative writing at Columbia University.

Design and Layout by Christine Innamorato

Consulting Editor: Michele I. Drohan

Photo Credits

Photo on p.14 by Ethan Zindler; p.16 by John Bentham; p.20 by Peter Russell Clemens/International Stock; pp. 29, 31 by Ira Fox; p. 30 by Eric Pearle/FPG International; pp. 39, 48 by Seth Dinnerman; pp. 44, 52 by Skjold Photographs; all other photos by Pablo Maldonado.